Cambridge Primary

Hodder Cambridge Primary

Maths

Workbook

Stage 1

Paul Wrangles

Series editors: Mike Askew
and Paul Broadbent

HODDER
EDUCATION
AN HACHETTE UK COMPANY

Acknowledgements

With warm thanks to Jennifer Peek for her help in shaping and developing this title.

The Publisher is extremely grateful to the following schools for their comments and feedback during the development of this series:
Avalon Heights World Private School, Ajman
The Oxford School, Dubai
Al Amana Private School, Sharjah
British International School, Ajman
Wesgreen International School, Sharjah
As Seeb International School, Al Khoud.

Although every effort has been made to ensure that website addresses are correct at time of going to press, Hodder Education cannot be held responsible for the content of any website mentioned in this book. It is sometimes possible to find a relocated web page by typing in the address of the home page for a website in the URL window of your browser.

Hachette UK's policy is to use papers that are natural, renewable and recyclable products and made from wood grown in sustainable forests. The logging and manufacturing processes are expected to conform to the environmental regulations of the country of origin.

Orders: please contact Bookpoint Ltd, 130 Milton Park, Abingdon, Oxon OX14 4SB. Telephone: (44) 01235 827720. Fax: (44) 01235 400454. Lines are open from 9.00–5.00, Monday to Saturday, with a 24 hour message answering service. You can also order through our website www.hoddereducation.com

© Paul Wrangles 2017

Published by Hodder Education

An Hachette UK Company

Carmelite House, 50 Victoria Embankment, London EC4Y 0DZ

Impression number   11

Year   2021

Cover illustration by Steve Evans

Illustrations by John Dickens and Jeanne du Plessis

Typeset in FS Albert 17/19 by DTP Impressions

Printed in Great Britain by Ashford Colour Press Ltd.

A catalogue record for this title is available from the British Library
9781471884566

Contents

Unit 1 Number and problem solving

Can you remember?

Match the questions and answers.

1 3 add 1 is _____.

2 6 add 3 is _____.

3 7 add 3 is _____.

4 10 take away 5 is _____.

5 10 take away 3 is _____.

6 10 take away 2 is _____.

a [5]   b [8]   c [4]   d [10]   e [9]   f [7]

Counting

1 Start with 1.
Join the dots
in order.
Say each number
out loud.

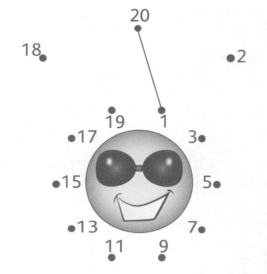

2 How many are there?

a

b

3 Draw 12 bananas.   Draw 18 apples.

4 Trace the numbers. Then match the numbers with their names.

six	1	11	seventeen
three	2	12	twenty
one	3	13	fourteen
five	4	14	fifteen
seven	5	15	nineteen
ten	6	16	eighteen
nine	7	17	eleven
two	8	18	sixteen
eight	9	19	twelve
four	10	20	thirteen

Comparing numbers

a Count and write the numbers.

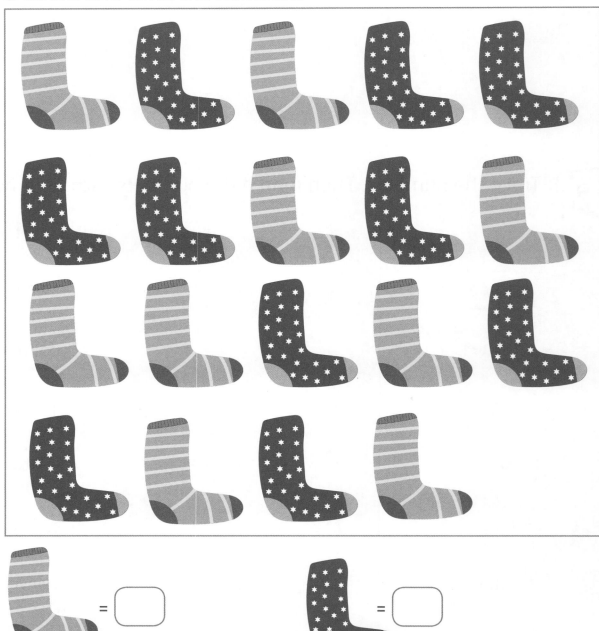

b Circle the sock that has **more**.

2 Which is the larger number?

a

6   9

b

13   10

c

17   18

d

20   16

3 Count each group of cubes. Order them from smallest to largest.

a

Smallest   Largest

b

Smallest   Largest

Addition and subtraction

1 Use counters to complete the number sentences.

a

⬤ ⬤ ⬤   ⬤ ⬤

⬜ and ⬜ make ⬜.

b

⬤ ⬤ ⬤ ⬤   ⬤ ⬤ ⬤

⬜ and ⬜ make ⬜.

c

⬤ ⬤ ⬤ ⬤ ⬤   ⬤ ⬤ ⬤

⬜ and ⬜ make ⬜.

2 Use cubes to complete the number sentences.

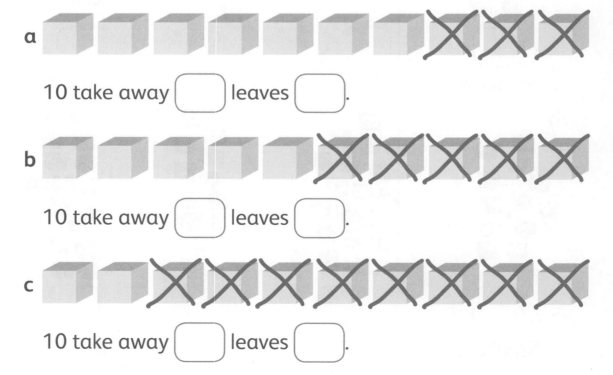

a

10 take away ⬜ leaves ⬜.

b

10 take away ⬜ leaves ⬜.

c

10 take away ⬜ leaves ⬜.

3 Cross out the balloons to show how many pop. Say how many balloons are left.

a 4 balloons pop

10 take away 4 ⟶ ☐.

b 6 balloons pop

10 take away 6 ⟶ ☐.

c 9 balloons pop

10 take away 9 ⟶ ☐.

4 Count **on** or **back** on the number line. Start with the larger number each time.

1 2 3 4 5 6 7 8 9 10 11 12 13 14 15 16 17 18 19 20

a 2 more than 11 makes ☐.

b 2 more than 12 makes ☐.

c 13 add 2 makes ☐.

d 14 add 2 makes ☐.

e 2 less than 10 is ☐.

f 2 less than 11 is ☐.

g 12 take away 2 leaves ☐.

h 13 take away 2 leaves ☐.

Self-assessment

Unit 1 Number and problem solving

😃	I understand this well.
😐	I understand this, but I need more practice.
🙁	I do not understand this.

I need more help with …

_____

_____

_____

Learning objectives	😃	😐	🙁
I can say numbers to 20 in order.			
I know how to write most numbers up to 20.			
I can count up to 20 objects.			
I can compare two numbers up to 20 and say which number is bigger.			
I can put numbers up to 20 in order.			
I can put two sets together to find the total.			
I can use objects to take away a small number from a number up to 10.			
I can use counters or a number line to find the number that is 2 more or 2 less.			

Unit 2 Geometry and problem solving

Can you remember?

Draw a line to match the shape names with these shapes.

1 cube **2** circle **3** cone **4** rectangle **5** triangle **6** cylinder

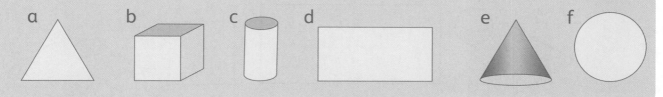

Patterns and shapes

1 Match each shape name to the right shape.

circle   triangle   rectangle   square

2 What shapes can you see in this picture?

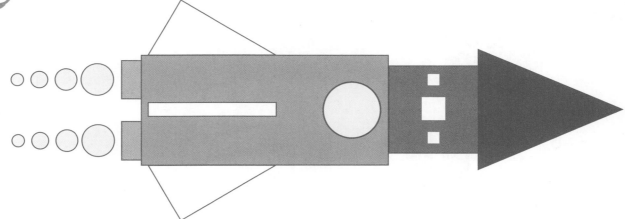

a There are ☐ squares.   **b** There are ☐ triangles.

c There are ☐ circles.   **d** There are ☐ rectangles.

11

Colour these shapes:
- Circles ——→ red
- Squares ——→ blue
- Triangles ——→ yellow

The shapes not coloured are all _____.

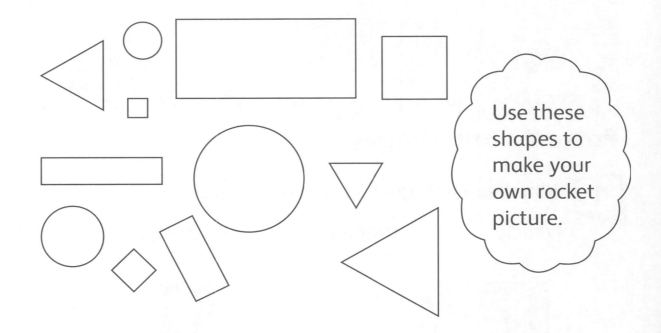

Use these shapes to make your own rocket picture.

 Draw the next three shapes in each pattern.

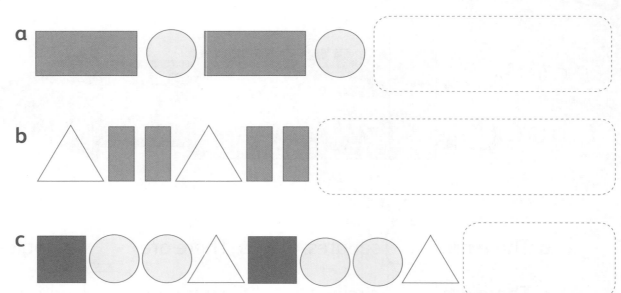

a

b

c

Tick (✓) the pictures that have symmetry.

a 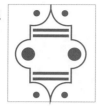 ◯

b ◯

c  ◯

d ◯

e  ◯

f  ◯

Making shapes

 Draw lines to match the shape names and shapes.

a pyramid

b sphere

c cube

d cone

e cylinder

f cuboid

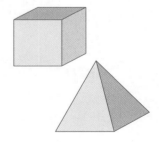

Count how many there are of each shape.

	Shape					
	Cube	Pyramid	Sphere	Cone	Cuboid	Cylinder
How many?						

 Sort the shapes.

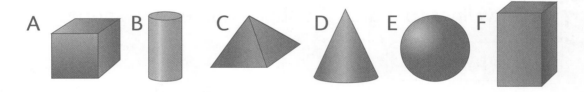

Shapes with a square face	Shapes with no square faces

Match each shape to the correct child. Complete the table.

A

The faces of my shape are all squares.

 B

My shape has no flat faces. It is curved all the way around.

C

My shape has faces that are circles at both ends.

 E

My shape has a circle face at only one end.

D

My shape has some faces that are triangles.

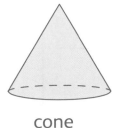

cone

cube

cylinder

pyramid

sphere

Child	Shape
A	
B	
C	
D	
E	

Self-assessment

Unit 2 Geometry and problem solving

I understand this well.

I understand this, but I need more practice.

I do not understand this.

I need more help with ...

_____

_____

_____

Learning objectives			
I can name most of the 2-D shapes that I see in my classroom.			
I can sort shapes by looking at them.			
I can use 2-D shapes to make patterns and pictures.			
I can use a mirror to make a reflection.			
I can use 3-D shapes to make patterns and models.			
I can name most of the 3-D shapes that I see in my classroom.			
I can see the 2-D shapes on the faces of solid 3-D shapes.			

Unit 3 Number and problem solving

Can you remember?

Circle the bigger number each time.

1 [4] or [7] ?   **2** [8] or [3] ?   **3** [13] or [6] ?

4 [15] or [18] ?   **5** [16] or [20] ?   **6** [19] or [11] ?

Numbers to 20

1 Write the missing numbers.

(1) (2) (3) (   ) (   ) (   ) (7) (   ) (   ) (10)

(11) (   ) (   ) (   ) (   ) (16) (17) (18) (   ) (   )

How many missing numbers are there? [   ]

2 Circle the bigger number. Use the number line to help you.

0 1 2 3 4 5 6 7 8 9 10 11 12 13 14 15 16 17 18 19 20

a (7) (10)   **b** (11) (9)

c (17) (14)   **d** (18) (20)

e (5) (16)   **f** (6) (15)

3 Roll a spinner three times.

For each number on the spinner, put that amount of counters onto the grid.

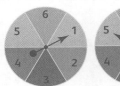

Show the total on the number line.

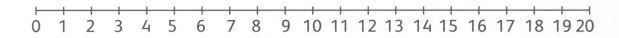

0 1 2 3 4 5 6 7 8 9 10 11 12 13 14 15 16 17 18 19 20

4 Colour the biggest number each time.

a 16   13   b 12   19

c 12   18   15   d 14   7   11

Addition and subtraction

1 Draw lines to join the numbers that make ten.

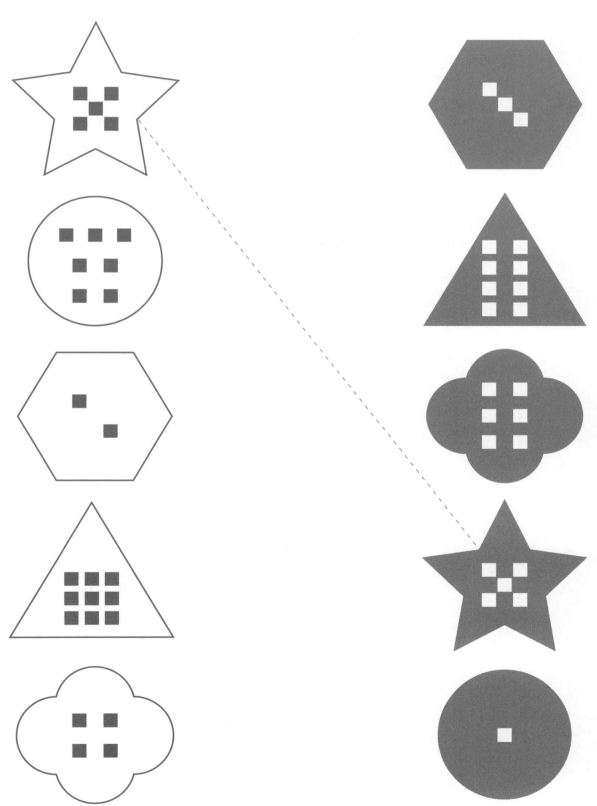

Colour the circles on the tens frames to show **different** ways to make ten. Use two colours.

a

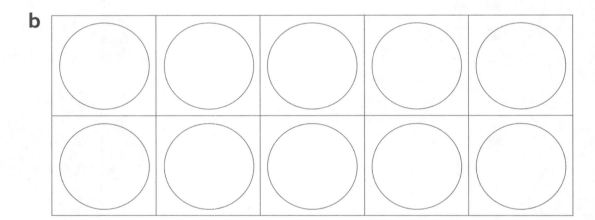

_____ and _____ make 10.

b

_____ and _____ make 10.

c

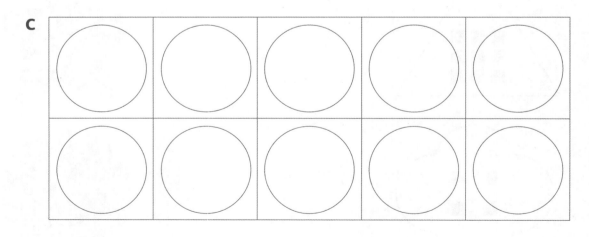

_____ and _____ make 10.

3 Count on to add these numbers. Colour the block you end on.

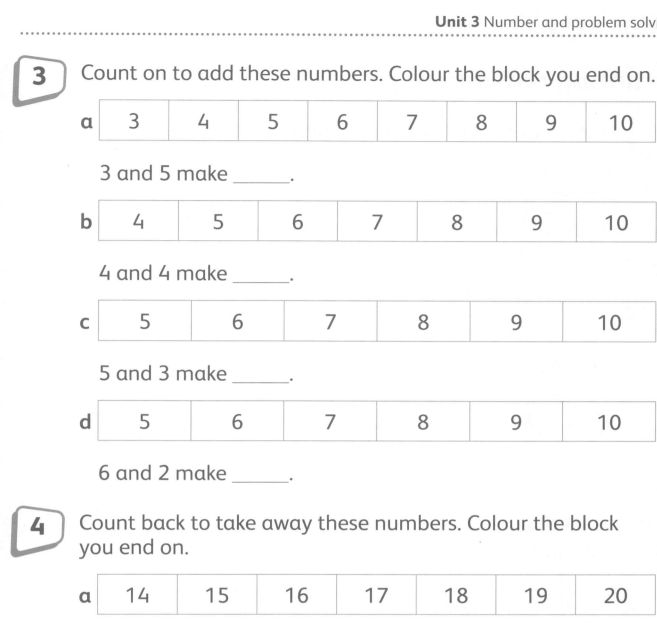

a

| 3 | 4 | 5 | 6 | 7 | 8 | 9 | 10 |

3 and 5 make _____.

b

| 4 | 5 | 6 | 7 | 8 | 9 | 10 |

4 and 4 make _____.

c

| 5 | 6 | 7 | 8 | 9 | 10 |

5 and 3 make _____.

d

| 5 | 6 | 7 | 8 | 9 | 10 |

6 and 2 make _____.

4 Count back to take away these numbers. Colour the block you end on.

a

| 14 | 15 | 16 | 17 | 18 | 19 | 20 |

19 take away 4 is _____.

b

| 14 | 15 | 16 | 17 | 18 | 19 | 20 |

18 take away 4 is _____.

c

| 12 | 13 | 14 | 15 | 16 | 17 | 18 |

17 take away 4 is _____.

d

| 12 | 13 | 14 | 15 | 16 | 17 | 18 |

16 take away 4 is _____.

Counting patterns

 Draw counters to double each number.

a Double 4 is _____.

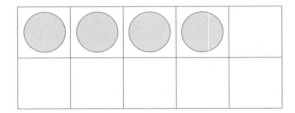

b Double 5 is _____.

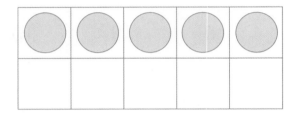

c Double 7 is _____.

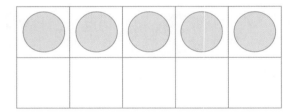 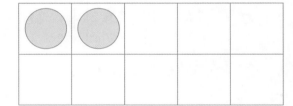

d Double 10 is _____.

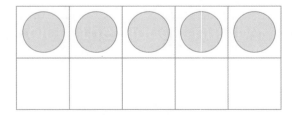 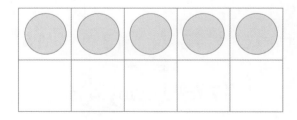

Estimate each number. Then count to check.

a

My estimate is ⬜.

The actual number is ⬜.

b

My estimate is ⬜.

The actual number is ⬜.

 Take a handful of counters.
Estimate the number of counters you have.
Then count to check.

My estimate is ⬜.　　The actual number is ⬜.

4 Complete these patterns.

Count in 1s.

a 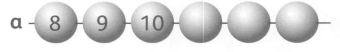 8 9 10

b 15 16

c 20 19

Count in 10s.

d  10 20 30

e 40 50

f 60 50

Count in 2s.

g 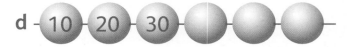 2 4 6

h 10 12

i 16 14

5 Count and say the numbers. Colour in each number you say on the number track.

a Count in ones from 1.

| 1 | 2 | 3 | 4 | 5 | 6 | 7 | 8 | 9 | 10 | 11 | 12 | 13 | 14 | 15 | 16 | 17 | 18 | 19 | 20 |

b Count in tens from 10.

| 1 | 2 | 3 | 4 | 5 | 6 | 7 | 8 | 9 | 10 | 11 | 12 | 13 | 14 | 15 | 16 | 17 | 18 | 19 | 20 |

c Count in twos from 2.

| 1 | 2 | 3 | 4 | 5 | 6 | 7 | 8 | 9 | 10 | 11 | 12 | 13 | 14 | 15 | 16 | 17 | 18 | 19 | 20 |

Self-assessment

Unit 3 Number and problem solving

😊 I understand this well.

😐 I understand this, but I need more practice.

☹️ I do not understand this.

I need more help with …

_____

_____

_____

Learning objectives	😊	😐	☹️
I know how to write numbers up to 20.			
I know where numbers up to 20 go on a number line.			
I can count up to 20 objects.			
I can compare numbers up to 20 and say which is bigger.			
I know some pairs of numbers that total 10.			
I can count on and back to add and subtract a number on a number line.			
I can use the +, − and = signs when I add and subtract.			
I can estimate the number in a group of up to 20 objects and check by counting.			
I can work out doubles of numbers to 10.			
I can count on and back in ones and tens.			
I am beginning to count in twos.			

Unit 4 Measure and problem solving

Can you remember?

Write these days of the week in the right order.

Friday	_____
Tuesday	_____
Saturday	_____
Wednesday	_____
Sunday	_____
Monday	_____
Thursday	_____

Money

 Estimate how many there are of each coin.
Then count to find out.

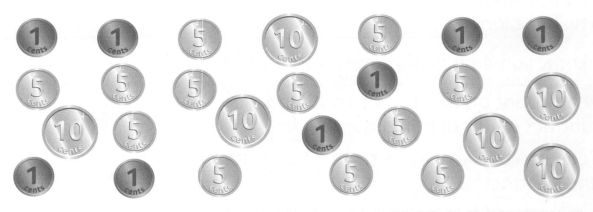

Coin	I estimate that there are ___.	I counted that there are ___.
a 1 cent		
b 5 cents		
c 10 cents		

How many coins are there **altogether**? ☐

2 Make these totals using 1 cent coins.

a 4 cents

b 9 cents

3 Estimate the amount of money in the purse.
Then count to check.

My estimate is ☐ cents.

The actual amount is ☐ cents.

Draw how you can make 6 cents using the coins in the purse.

Measures

1 **a** Measure the line using cubes. Draw and measure a line that is longer.

_____ ( ) cubes

( ) cubes

b Use cubes to make longer and shorter trains.
Draw the trains that you make.

My shorter train:

My longer train:

2 Tick (✔) the heaviest toy.

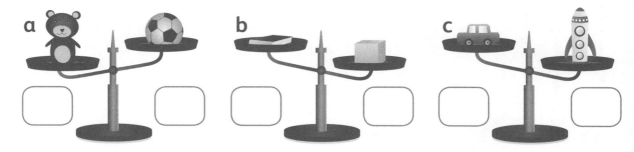

a   b   c

3 Tick (✔) the heaviest fruit in each group.

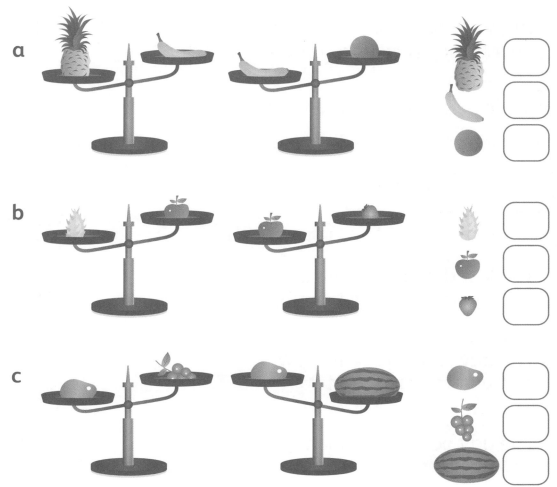

a

b

c

4 Take three boxes. Call them A, B and C.
How many cubes do you need to fill each box?
Complete the table.

Box	Number of cubes
A	
B	
C	

a Which box holds the most?   Box ⬚

b Which box holds the least?   Box ⬚

Time

1 Draw lines to join the sentences with a day of the week. Some of them may have the same answer!

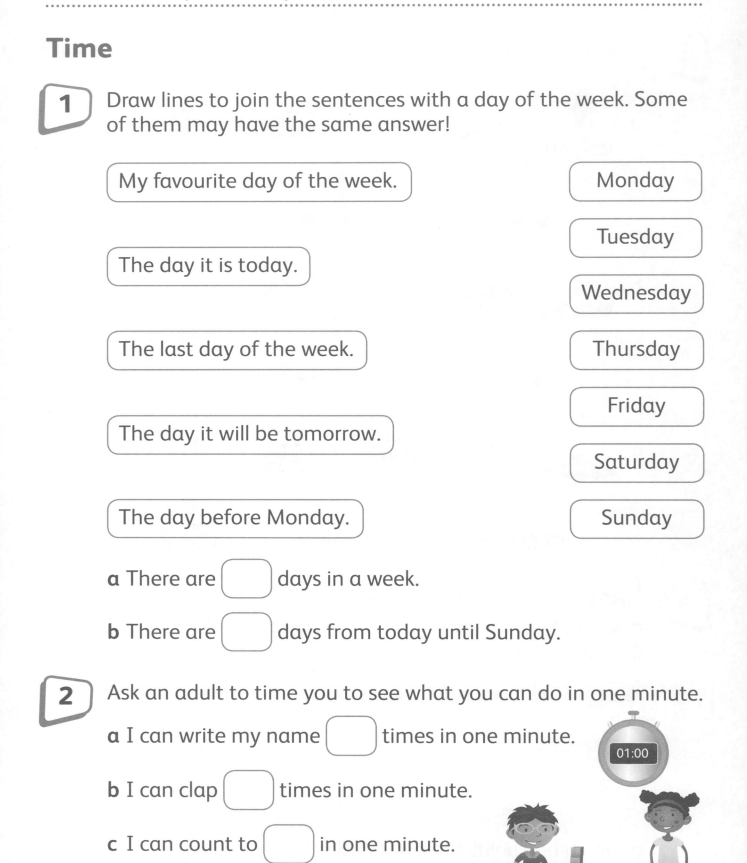

My favourite day of the week.

The day it is today.

The last day of the week.

The day it will be tomorrow.

The day before Monday.

Monday

Tuesday

Wednesday

Thursday

Friday

Saturday

Sunday

a There are ☐ days in a week.

b There are ☐ days from today until Sunday.

2 Ask an adult to time you to see what you can do in one minute.

a I can write my name ☐ times in one minute.

b I can clap ☐ times in one minute.

c I can count to ☐ in one minute.

d I can hop ☐ times in one minute.

01:00

Self-assessment

Unit 4 Measure and problem solving

🙂 I understand this well.

😐 I understand this, but I need more practice.

☹️ I do not understand this.

I need more help with ...

_____

_____

_____

Learning objectives	🙂	😐	☹️
I can recognise and name some coins.			
I can make totals up to 10 cents with 1 cent coins.			
I can estimate how much money I have.			
I can compare the lengths of more than two objects.			
I can use a balance to compare the weights of more than two objects.			
I can compare the capacities of two or more containers.			
I know the days of the week.			
I can use a timer to count how many jumps I can do.			

Unit 6 Number and problem solving

Can you remember?

1 Double 3 is ☐.

2 Double 5 is ☐.

3 Double 2 is ☐.

4 Double 1 is ☐.

5 Double 4 is ☐.

6 Double 6 is ☐.

Counting patterns

1 Count on the number track. Colour in the right word.

1	2	3	4	5	6	7	8	9	10	11	12	13	14	15	16	17	18	19	20

a Two more than 8 is [ten] [twelve].

b Two less than 16 is [twelve] [fourteen].

c The numbers I have coloured in are [odd] [even] numbers.

2 Count the cubes. Colour in the right word.

a Two more than 14 is [sixteen] [eighteen].

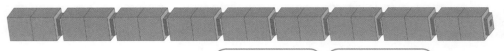

b Two less than 20 is [sixteen] [eighteen].

3 Count and write the missing numbers.

2 4 6 ⬜ ⬜ ⬜ 14 ⬜ 18 ⬜

1 3 5 ⬜ ⬜ 11 ⬜ ⬜ ⬜ 19

What is the same and what is different about these patterns?

_____

_____

4 Draw double the amount for each object.

Object	Double the amount

Numbers

 1 Write **more** or **less**.

0	1	2	3	4	5	6	7	8	9	10	11	12	13	14	15	16	17	18	19	20

a 5 is _____ than 4.

b 6 is _____ than 8.

c 9 is _____ than 11.

d 13 is _____ than 15.

e 18 is _____ than 16.

2 Match the number sentences with the right answer.
a 10 more than 10
b 10 less than 40
c 10 less than 20
d 10 more than 50
e 10 less than 50
f 10 more than 40

3 Split these numbers into tens and ones.

a 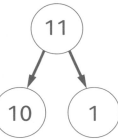   **b** 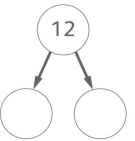   **c**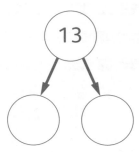

d 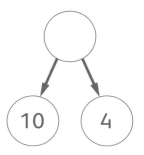   **e** 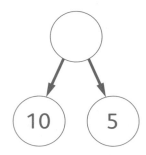   **f**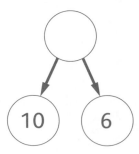

Use this tens rod and these cubes to make different numbers.

Draw tens rods and cubes to show the numbers you made.

Write the number.

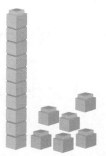

My drawing	What number does it show?
□□□□□□□□□□ □ □	12

Self-assessment

Unit 6 Number and problem solving

😊 I understand this well.

😐 I understand this, but I need more practice.

☹ I do not understand this.

I need more help with …

_____

_____

_____

Learning objectives	😊	😐	☹
I can work out doubles of numbers.			
I am beginning to recognise odd and even numbers when I count in twos.			
I can count on and back in tens.			
I can compare numbers and say the number that is **more** or **less**.			
I can say the number that is 10 more or 10 less than 10, 20 or 30.			
I am beginning to partition numbers into tens and ones.			

Unit 7 Handling data and problem solving

Can you remember?

What are the next two shapes in each pattern?

a ▢ △ ▢ △ _____

b ▭ ▭ ○ ▭ ▭ ○ _____

c ○ ▢ ▢ △ ○ ▢ ▢ △ _____

Sorting objects and shapes

a Colour the shapes with one curved side in yellow.
b Colour the shapes with three sides in blue.
c Colour the shapes with four sides in red.

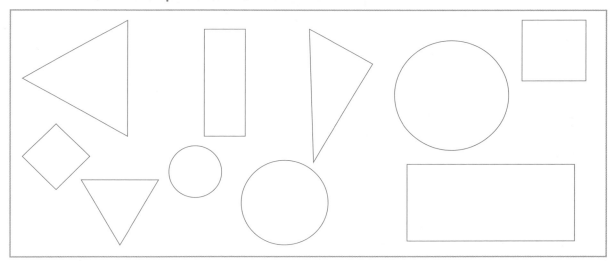

2 Use these words to complete the sentences.

squares	rectangles	triangles	circles

a The yellow shapes are all _____.

b The blue shapes are all _____.

c The red shapes are all _____ and _____.

3 Draw your own shapes to match the headings in the table.

4 straight sides	1 curved side	straight and curved sides	3 sides

4 Sort these shapes into the Venn diagram.
Write the number for where you think each shape belongs.

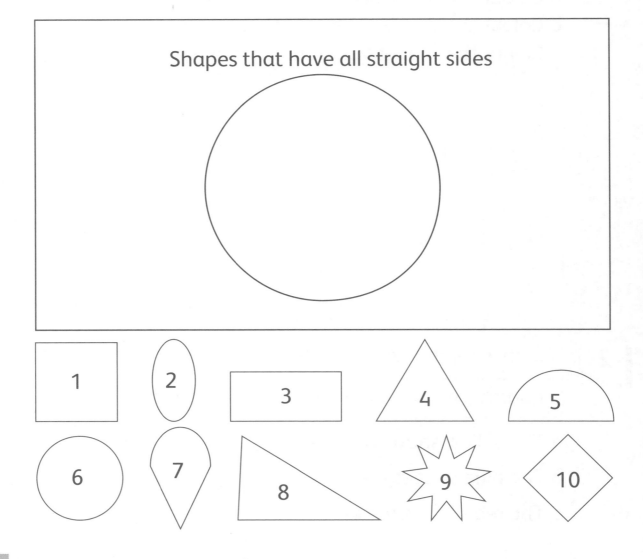

Shapes that have all straight sides

Pictograms

a Take three handfuls of coloured counters.
Sort them so that you can see how many there are of each colour.

b Colour and label this pictogram to show the number you took of each different colour.

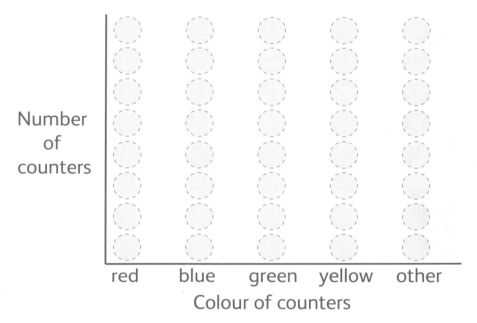

c Count the circles for each colour. Write the answer in the table.

Colour	Number of counters
Red	
Blue	
Green	
Yellow	
Other	

d There were ⬭ MORE ⬭ FEWER red counters than yellow counters.

There were ⬭ MORE ⬭ FEWER blue counters than green counters.

2 Lev is in the park. He can see these things that begin with the letter **b**.

He can see **8 balls**, **1 bicycle**, **5 bins**, **2 benches** and **5 birds**.

a Complete the pictogram to show how many of each thing Lev sees.

Objects in the park beginning with 'b'

◯ = 1 object

b Use the words in the pictogram to complete these sentences.

Lev sees more _____ than _____.

Lev sees less _____ than _____.

c How many things can Lev see altogether? ◯

Self-assessment

Unit 7 Handling data and problem solving

😊 I understand this well.

😐 I understand this, but I need more practice.

☹️ I do not understand this.

I need more help with …

_____

_____

_____

Learning objectives	😊	😐	☹️
I can sort objects and shapes on a Venn diagram.			
I can describe 2-D shapes and talk about their sides.			
I can describe 3-D shapes and talk about their faces.			
I can show numbers of objects in a pictogram and say how many there are.			
I can answer questions about my pictogram.			

Unit 8 Number and problem solving

Can you remember?

Write the answers.

1 5 + 2 = ☐

2 7 − 5 = ☐

3 6 + 3 = ☐

4 8 − 3 = ☐

5 6 + 4 = ☐

6 9 − 7 = ☐

7 8 + 6 = ☐

8 12 − 4 = ☐

Addition

1 Build the cube chains. Draw the cubes. Then write the answer.

a 6 cubes and 5 cubes

6 + 5 = ☐

b 6 cubes and 6 cubes

6 + 6 = ☐

c 6 cubes and 7 cubes

6 + 7 = ☐

d 6 cubes and 8 cubes

6 + 8 = ☐

e 6 cubes and 9 cubes

6 + 9 = ☐

2 Show that both additions have the same total.
Use two different colours.

a

$2 + 8 =$ ⬡ $8 + 2 =$ ⬡

b

$4 + 7 =$ ⬡ $7 + 4 =$ ⬡

c

$4 + 8 =$ ⬡ $8 + 4 =$ ⬡

d

$9 + 4 =$ ⬡ $4 + 9 =$ ⬡

3 a   b

$7 = 4 +$ _____ $9 = 4 +$ _____

$7 =$ _____ $+ 4$ $9 =$ _____ $+ 4$

c   d

$11 = 4 +$ _____ $13 = 4 +$ _____

$11 =$ _____ $+ 4$ $13 =$ _____ $+ 4$

Subtraction

1 Use a number line to count back from the bigger number.

a 5 – 3 = ☐

b 15 – 3 = ☐

c 6 – 3 = ☐

d 16 – 3 = ☐

e 7 – 3 = ☐

f 17 – 3 = ☐

2 Answer these questions to show how subtraction and addition facts are linked.

a

9 – 3 = _____

6 + 3 = _____

b

10 – 2 = _____

8 + 2 = _____

c

12 – 7 = _____

5 + 7 = _____

3 What is the difference between these cube towers?

a 10 − 8 = ☐

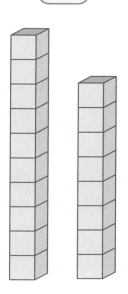

b 12 − 6 = ☐

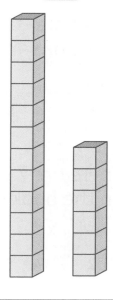

c 13 − 8 = ☐

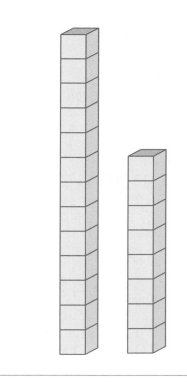

d 14 − 9 = ☐

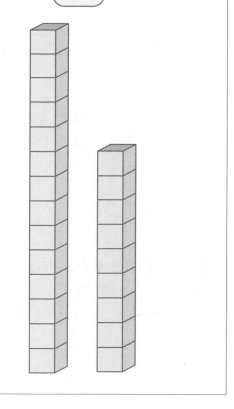

Addition and subtraction

1 Write **+** or **−** for these to show if it is an addition or a subtraction. Show each one on the number line.

a There are 8 birds in a tree. 4 of them fly away. There are 4 birds left.

b There are 7 books on a book case. Sofia puts another 5 books on the book case. There are now 12 books altogether.

c A pizza takes 10 minutes to cook. 6 minutes go by. There are now only 4 minutes left.

d There are 12 people on a bus. 3 more people get on the bus. There are now 15 people altogether.

2 Write **+** or **−** for each answer.

a 5 ☐ 5 = 10   **b** 9 ☐ 2 = 7   **c** 12 ☐ 5 = 7

d 11 ☐ 7 = 18   **e** 13 ☐ 3 = 10   **f** 14 ☐ 5 = 19

3   Use this number line to help you solve these word problems.

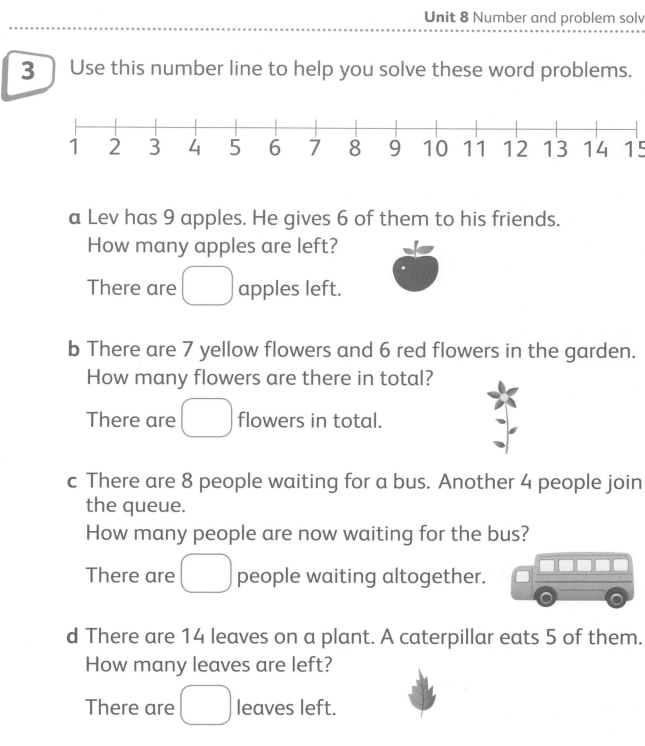

a Lev has 9 apples. He gives 6 of them to his friends.
How many apples are left?

There are ⬚ apples left.

b There are 7 yellow flowers and 6 red flowers in the garden.
How many flowers are there in total?

There are ⬚ flowers in total.

c There are 8 people waiting for a bus. Another 4 people join the queue.
How many people are now waiting for the bus?

There are ⬚ people waiting altogether.

d There are 14 leaves on a plant. A caterpillar eats 5 of them.
How many leaves are left?

There are ⬚ leaves left.

e Maya's friend has 3 books in Maya's bag. Maya has 4 more books in her bag.

There are ⬚ books in Maya's bag.

Self-assessment

Unit 8 Number and problem solving

😊 I understand this well.

😐 I understand this, but I need more practice.

☹️ I do not understand this.

I need more help with …

_____

_____

_____

Learning objectives	😊	😐	☹️
I can put two sets of cubes together to add them.			
I know that 4 + 3 is the same as 3 + 4 and they both total 7.			
I can check if my addition is right by adding it in a different order.			
I can count back to subtract a number on a number line.			
I can work out the difference between two numbers by comparing cube towers.			
I can check if an answer to a take away sum is right by adding the answer to the smaller number.			
I can use the +, − and = signs when I add and subtract.			
I know if I need to add or subtract to solve a problem.			

Can you remember?

How much money do you have?

1 ① + ① + ① + ① ☐ cents

2 ① + ① + ⑤ ☐ cents

3 ⑤ + ⑤ ☐ cents

4 ⑩ + ① + ① ☐ cents

5 ⑩ + ⑤ ☐ cents

Money

1 Make each total. You can use any of these coins.

a 4 cents

b 10 cents

c 12 cents

d 20 cents

Make each amount in two different ways.

Example:
5 cents

a 6 cents

b 10 cents

c 13 cents

d 15 cents

Measures

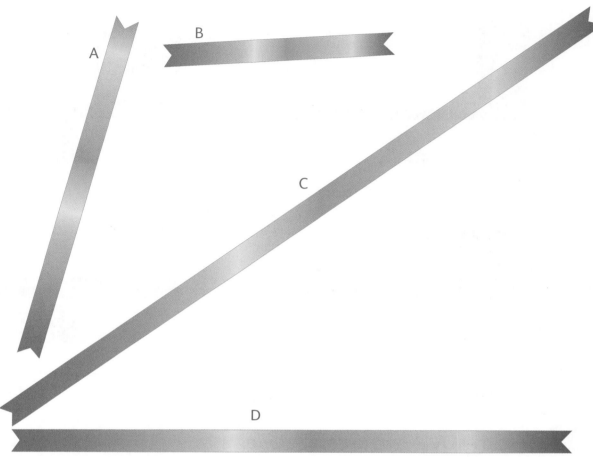

1 Measure these pieces of ribbon using counters.
How many counters will you use for each ribbon?

a Ribbon A is ☐ counters long.

b Ribbon B is ☐ counters long.

c Ribbon C is ☐ counters long.

c Ribbon D is ☐ counters long.

2 Use **longer** or **shorter** to complete these sentences.

a Ribbon A is ☐ than Ribbon D.

b Ribbon B is ☐ than Ribbon C.

3 Count the weights to see how heavy each object is.

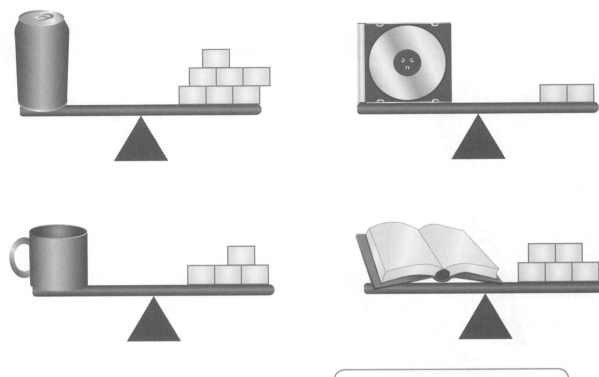

a Is the mug or the book heavier?

b Is the DVD or the can heavier?

4 Take four bowls. Call them A, B, C and D.

a How many cups of water do you need to fill each bowl? Complete the table.

Box	Number of cups of water
A	
B	
C	
D	

b Does Bowl D hold MORE or LESS water than Bowl A?

c Which bowl holds the most water?   Bowl

d Which bowl holds the least water?   Bowl

Time

 Write the correct month of the year to complete these sentences. Some sentences may have the same answers!

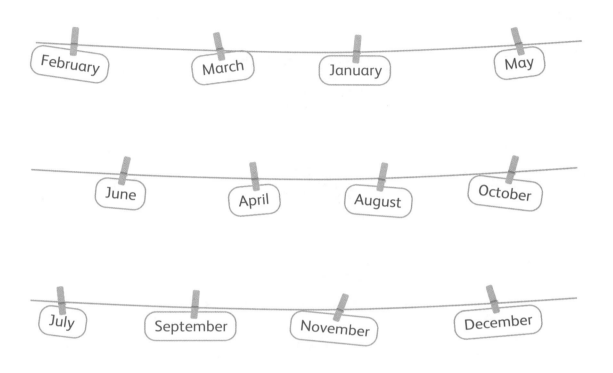

a The month we are in now is _____.

b The month that comes after July is _____.

c The last month of the year is _____.

d The month that comes before November is _____.

e The first month of the year is _____.

f The second month of the year is _____.

g My favourite month of the year is _____.

2 Look at these activities.

a Draw the hands on each clock to show the time.

five o'clock

two o'clock

eight o'clock

twelve o'clock

b Write 1 to 4 in the box for each picture to show the right order of the activities.

3 Match the clocks and times.

a

b

c

d

e

f

g

h

i

j

six o'clock

ten o'clock

four o'clock

one o'clock

two o'clock

seven o'clock

eleven o'clock

eight o'clock

nine o'clock

three o'clock

Self-assessment

Unit 9 Measure and problem solving

| I understand this well. | I understand this, but I need more practice. | I do not understand this. |

I need more help with …

_____

_____

_____

Learning objectives	😊	😐	🙁
I can recognise and name all coins.			
I can exchange coins to make matching amounts.			
I can find different ways to make 10 cents.			
I can use cubes to measure and compare the length of objects.			
I can use weights to balance a parcel.			
I can compare the capacities of more than two containers and put them in order.			
I know some of the months of the year.			
I can put events in order.			
I know that it is 3 o'clock when the big hand points to the 12 and the small hand points to the 3.			

Can you remember?

Complete these number patterns.

1 2   4   6   [ ]   [ ]   [ ]   [ ]   [ ]

2 10   20   30   [ ]   [ ]   [ ]   [ ]   [ ]

3 20   18   16   [ ]   [ ]   [ ]   [ ]   [ ]

4 100   90   80   [ ]   [ ]   [ ]   [ ]   [ ]

Counting patterns

1 Use the cubes in the grids to help you double each even number.

a   Double 2 is [ ].   b   Double 4 is [ ].

c   Double 6 is [ ].   d   Double 8 is [ ].

Double these odd numbers. What do you notice?

e   Double 1 is [ ].   f   Double 3 is [ ].

g   Double 5 is [ ].

h   Double 7 is [ ].

2 Write the missing numbers.

a Count in twos from 2. Colour each number in yellow.

b Count in tens from 10. Colour each number in red.

1	2	3	4	5	6	7	8	9	
11	12	13	14	15		17	18	19	20
21		23	24	25	26	27	28	29	
31	32	33	34	35	36	37		39	40
41	42	43		45	46	47	48	49	

3 Maya is counting in twos.

a She starts with the number 10 and stops when she gets to 20. She says, "These are all **even** numbers."

Is she right? Yes No

b Write down the numbers Maya says to show if she is right or wrong.

c Maya then starts on the number 100. She counts back in tens for four numbers. What number does she end on?

d Lev starts with the number 30. He counts forwards in tens for 5 numbers. He says the number 59.

Has he counted correctly? Yes No
Why do you think this?

4 Colour in the multiples.
a Colour the multiples of 2 in green.

| 12 | 6 | 9 | 25 | 14 | 3 | 10 | 17 |

b Colour the multiples of 10 in red.

(18) (10) (21) (13) (50) (30) (8) (20)

5 Read what the children are saying. Tick (✓) the two sentences that you think are true.

Multiples of 2 always end in a 2.

Multiples of 2 are always even numbers.

Multiples of 10 always end in a 0.

Multiples of 10 are always odd numbers.

Numbers

1 Write **more** or **less**.

a 5 is _____ than 9.

b 7 is _____ than 11.

c 8 is _____ than 6.

d 15 is _____ than 13.

e 17 is _____ than 20.

f 18 is _____ than 16.

2 What number belongs between these number pairs?

| 15 | 8 | 4 | 12 | 14 | 19 |

a 2 and 5 _____   b 14 and 16 _____

c 10 and 13 _____   d 17 and 20 _____

e 6 and 9 _____   f 12 and 15 _____

3 Write these numbers in order. Start with the smallest number.

| 17 | 3 | 14 | 9 | 5 | 10 | 12 |

4 Lev uses these cards to make three different numbers that are more than 10.

1 0 > 5 > 3 > 8 >

a What are the numbers Lev makes?

☐ ☐ ☐

Lev puts his numbers in order from smallest to largest.

b Which of his numbers comes 1st? ☐

c Which of his numbers comes 2nd? ☐

d Which of his numbers comes 3rd? ☐

Split these numbers into tens and ones.

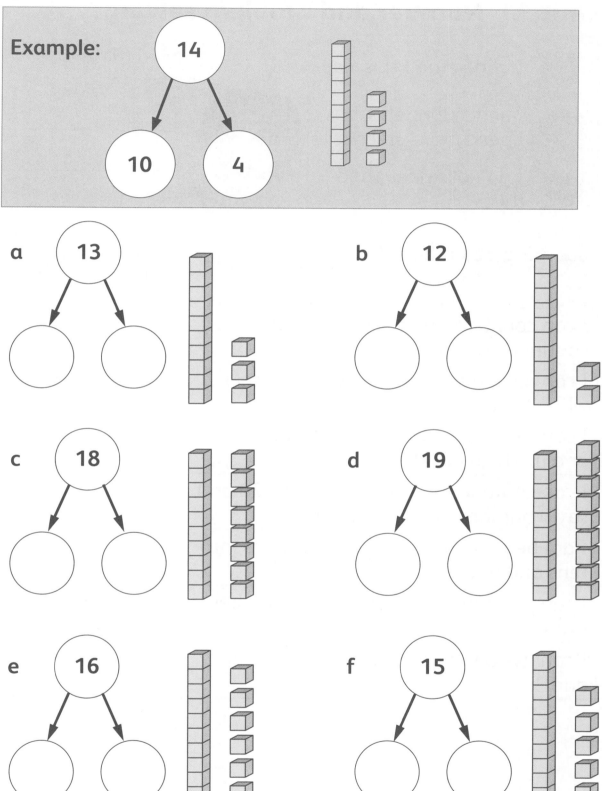

Self-assessment

Unit 11 Number and problem solving

I need more help with ...

_____

_____

_____

Learning objectives	😊	😐	☹
I can count on and back in tens and twos to continue patterns.			
I can recognise odd and even numbers when I count.			
I can tell you if a number is a multiple of 2 or a multiple of 10.			
I can compare two numbers up to 20 and say a number that is between them.			
I am beginning to partition numbers into tens and ones.			
I can put numbers in order on a number track.			
I can use ordinal numbers like 1st, 2nd and 3rd.			

Unit 12 Handling data and problem solving

Can you remember?

Complete these sentences.

1 A _____ has 4 sides all the same length.

2 A _____ has 4 sides and two of them are different lengths.

3 A _____ has 1 curved side.

Sorting numbers

1 Make each number out of cubes. Split them in two groups. Colour the squares to show the groups you made.

a

16 is an ┌ even ┐ ┌ odd ┐ number because I ┌ could ┐ ┌ could not ┐ sort it into two equal groups.

b

13 is an ┌ even ┐ ┌ odd ┐ number because I ┌ could ┐ ┌ could not ┐ sort it into two equal groups.

c

14 is an ┌ even ┐ ┌ odd ┐ number because I ┌ could ┐ ┌ could not ┐ sort it into two equal groups.

2 Play this game with a partner.

a Spin two spinners and add the numbers together.

If you can see the total on your grid of even numbers, colour in the number.

The winner is the first person to colour in a row of three even numbers.

2	4	6	8	10	12

Player 1

2	4	6	8	10	12

Player 2

b If you were playing this game with odd numbers, what are the five different odd numbers you could make using two spinners?

3 Look carefully at the numbers that have been sorted in this Carroll diagram.

A	B
6 10 12 18 2	11 5 15 17 9

a Write the rules for both sets of numbers.

Rule A : Numbers that are _____.

Rule B : Numbers that are _____.

b Write two more numbers that belong in Box A.

c Write two more numbers that belong in Box B.

Write the numbers in the right place on these Venn diagrams.

a

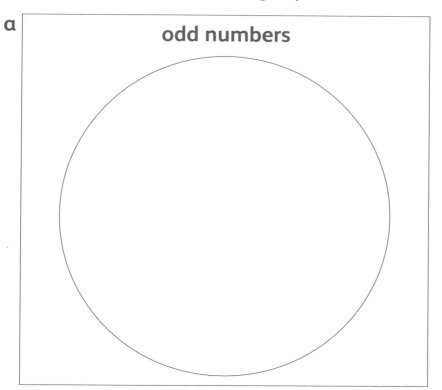

odd numbers

18
3
7   11
9
14
13
12
6
20
17
19
15

b

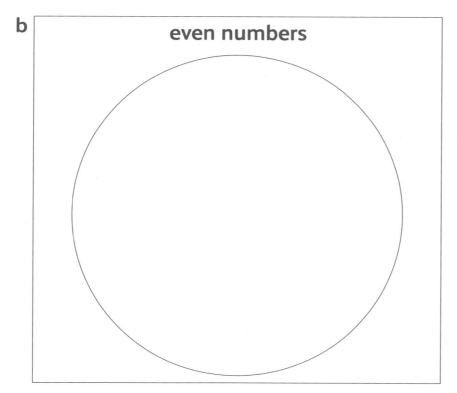

even numbers

18
3
7   11
9
14
13
12
6
20
17
19
15

What do you notice about the two Venn diagrams?

_____

Sorting shapes

1 Draw these shapes in the table.
Tick (✓) the right blocks to say what each shape is like.

square   triangle   rectangle   circle

Shape	How many sides?			What are the sides like?		Are the sides all the same length?		
	1	3	4	Straight	Curved	Yes	No	Sometimes

2 Sort these shapes into this Carroll diagram.
Write the letters for where they belong.

A 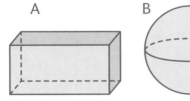   B   C 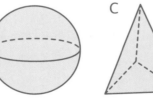   D   E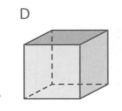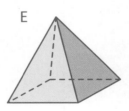

Has six faces	Does not have six faces

Block graphs

 Lev asked his class what vegetable they like best. This is what he found out:

Vegetable	Number of children who like it
carrot	5
potato	6
cabbage	1
broccoli	4
green beans	3

Show the results on this block graph.

Each square shows one child.

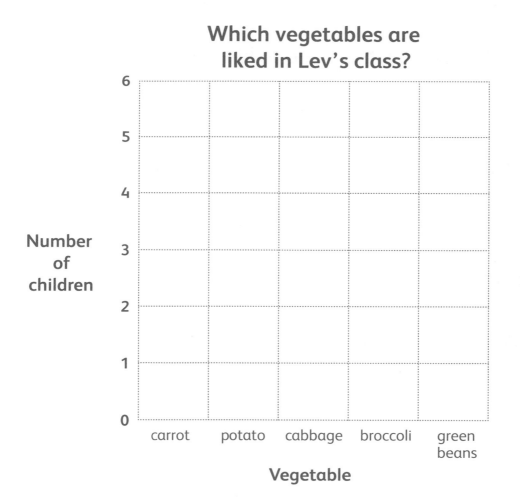

2 Answer these questions about the block graph.

a Which vegetable is the most popular?

_____

b Which vegetable is the least popular?

_____

How do you know?

_____

_____

c Which vegetable has three children who like it?

_____

d Which vegetable has five children who like it?

_____

e How many more children like carrots than cabbage?

f How many children did Lev ask altogether?
How do you know?

_____

_____

Self-assessment

Unit 12 Handling data and problem solving

😊 I understand this well.

😐 I understand this, but I need more practice.

☹ I do not understand this.

I need more help with …

_____

_____

_____

Learning objectives	😊	😐	☹
I can sort numbers on a Venn or Carroll diagram.			
I can work out if a number is an odd number or an even number.			
I can compare numbers up to 20 and say which is bigger or smaller.			
I can sort shapes in different ways on a Venn or Carroll diagram.			
I can describe 2-D shapes and talk about their sides and corners.			
I can describe 3-D shapes and show the number of faces.			
I can show numbers of objects in a block graph and say how many there are.			
I can answer questions about my block graph.			
I can explain how I worked out the answer to a question about my graph.			

Can you remember?

Match the number facts and answers.

| Half of 12 | Double 7 | Half of 20 | Double 6 | Half of 18 |

| 10 | 9 | 12 | 6 | 14 |

Addition and subtraction

 Lev has worked out these subtractions.
Check if his answers are right by adding the answer to the smaller number.

Example: 10 − 3 = 7   Check: 7 + 3 = 10

a 11 − 3 = 8   Check: ☐ + ☐ = ☐

b 14 − 5 = 9   Check: ☐ + ☐ = ☐

c 13 − 6 = 7   Check: ☐ + ☐ = ☐

d 16 − 7 = 9   Check: ☐ + ☐ = ☐

 Write the missing numbers.

How many more?

a 7 + ☐ = 14

b 12 + ☐ = 15

c 5 + ☐ = 20

How many to take away?

d 13 − ☐ = 6

e 17 − ☐ = 13

f 20 − ☐ = 9

3 In each of these additions there is a hidden 10.
Split up the second number to help you make ten.

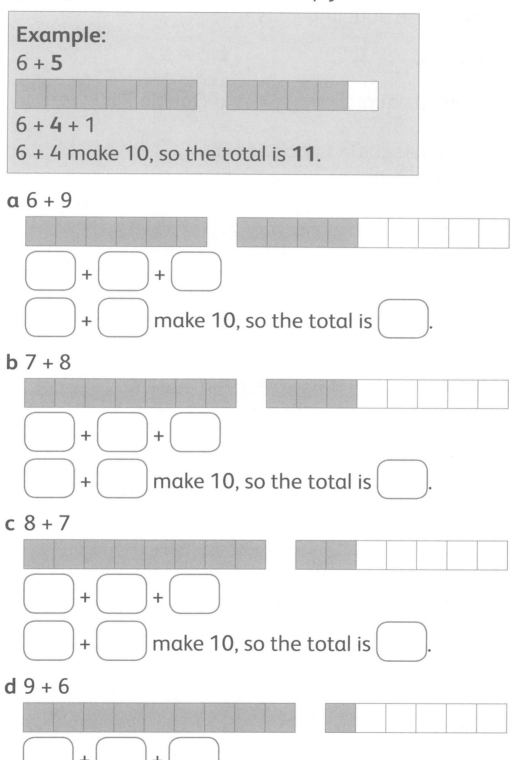

Example:
6 + 5

6 + **4** + 1
6 + 4 make 10, so the total is **11**.

a 6 + 9

◯ + ◯ + ◯

◯ + ◯ make 10, so the total is ◯.

b 7 + 8

◯ + ◯ + ◯

◯ + ◯ make 10, so the total is ◯.

c 8 + 7

◯ + ◯ + ◯

◯ + ◯ make 10, so the total is ◯.

d 9 + 6

◯ + ◯ + ◯

◯ + ◯ make 10, so the total is ◯.

Doubles and halves

1 Complete these doubling facts.

a Double 2 is ☐.   **b** 5 + 5 = ☐.

c Six doubled equals ☐.   **d** Double 7 is ☐.

2 Use two colours to find each answer.
Use red to show the doubling fact.
Then use blue to colour one more circle to show the near double.

a 4 + 5 = ☐

b 5 + 6 = ☐

c 6 + 7 = ☐

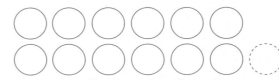

3 Use objects to make these numbers. Then share them into two equal groups to find half. Draw the two groups you make.

a Half of 12 is ☐.

b Half of 16 is ☐.

c Half of 18 is ☐.

d Half of 20 is ☐.

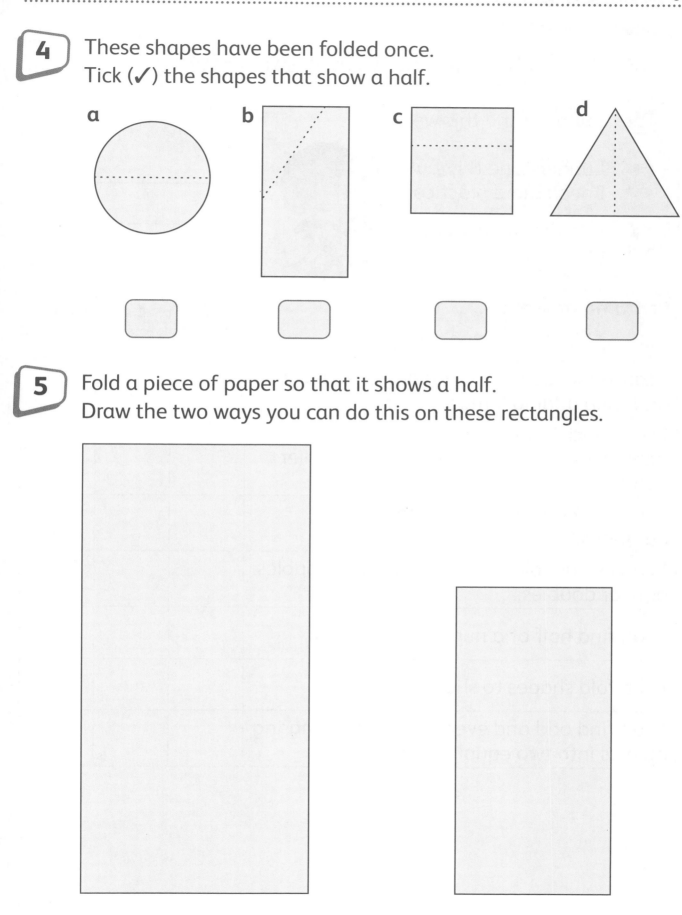

4 These shapes have been folded once.
Tick (✓) the shapes that show a half.

a   b   c   d

5 Fold a piece of paper so that it shows a half.
Draw the two ways you can do this on these rectangles.

Self-assessment

Unit 13   Number and problem solving

😀	I understand this well.
😐	I understand this, but I need more practice.
🙁	I do not understand this.

I need more help with …

_____

_____

_____

Learning objectives	😀	😐	🙁
I can work out 7 + 4 by adding 3 to make 10 and then adding 1 more.			
I can check if an answer to a take away is right by adding the answer to the smaller number.			
I can work out missing numbers in a number sentence.			
I can use doubles to work out other doubles or near doubles.			
I can find half of a number of objects.			
I can fold shapes to show halves.			
I can find odd and even numbers by sharing objects into two equal groups.			

Unit 14 Measure and problem solving

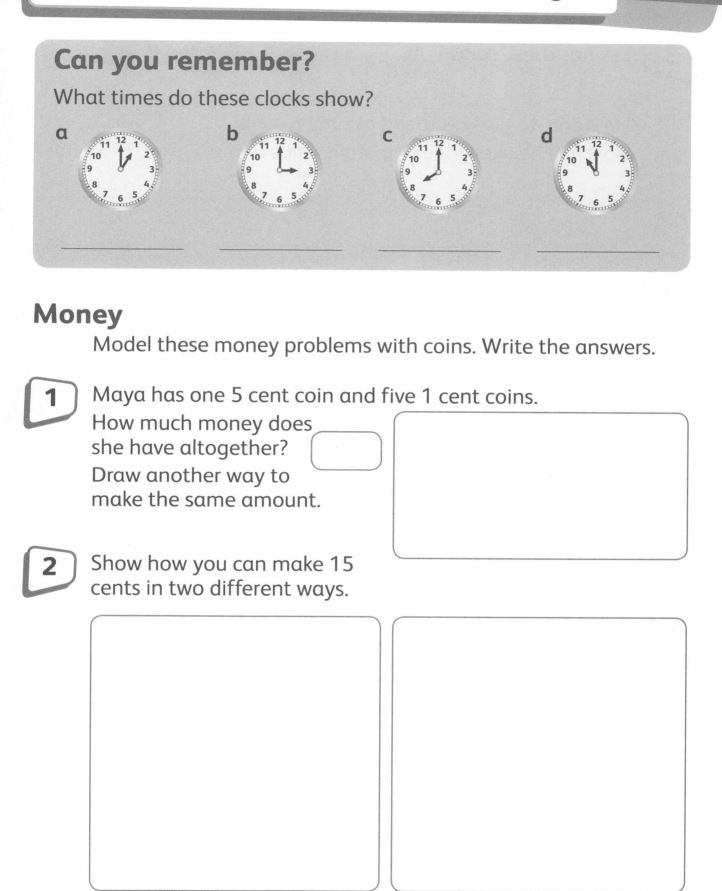

Can you remember?

What times do these clocks show?

a

b

c

d

_____ _____ _____ _____

Money

Model these money problems with coins. Write the answers.

1 Maya has one 5 cent coin and five 1 cent coins.
How much money does
she have altogether?
Draw another way to
make the same amount.

2 Show how you can make 15
cents in two different ways.

Lev has these coins.

He wants to give his friend exactly 8 cents.
How can he exchange one of his coins to make exactly 8 cents?

_____

_____

 Zara has three different coins.
Draw four different amounts she could have.

Measures

 Colour in the words that show the best way to measure these.

a The length of a sandwich: [hand spans] or [plastic counters]?

b The weight of a pencil case: [bricks] or [marbles]?

c The capacity of a bowl: [glasses] or [baths] of water?

d The length of a classroom: [paces] or [cubes]?

2 Read what the children are saying and answer the questions.

a

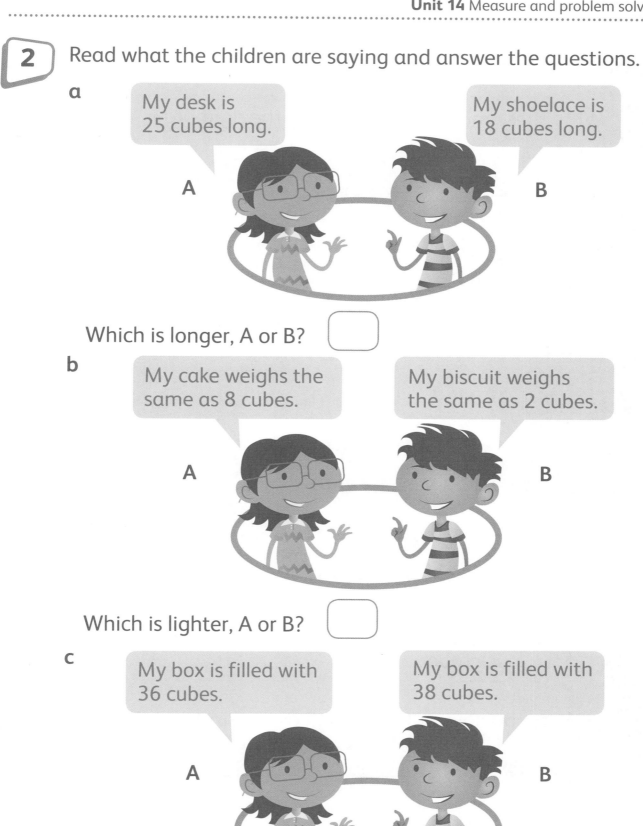

My desk is 25 cubes long.

My shoelace is 18 cubes long.

A

B

Which is longer, A or B?

b

My cake weighs the same as 8 cubes.

My biscuit weighs the same as 2 cubes.

A

B

Which is lighter, A or B?

c

My box is filled with 36 cubes.

My box is filled with 38 cubes.

A

B

Which holds more, A or B?

Time and movement

1 Write these months of the year in the right order.

June

November

September

February

December

August

July

January

May

March

April

October

_____

_____

_____

_____

_____

_____

_____

_____

_____

_____

_____

_____

2 **a** Write the days of the week in order. Start with Monday.

Monday _____ _____ _____

_____ _____ _____

b Which day comes after Thursday? [   ]

c Which day comes before Wednesday? [   ]

3 Draw these times on the clock faces.

a
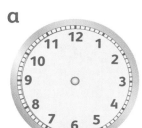
three o'clock

b

ten o'clock

c

six o'clock

d

nine o'clock

4 Use these words to describe how the square (■) can move through the maze:

> left   right   forwards   backwards

In ■

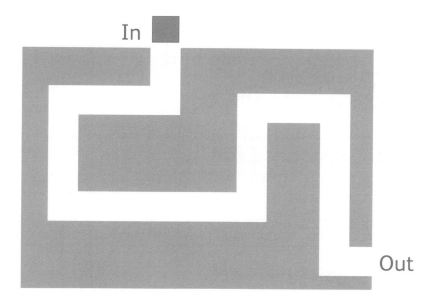

Out

Self-assessment

Unit 14 Measure and problem solving

😀	I understand this well.
😐	I understand this, but I need more practice.
☹️	I do not understand this.

I need more help with …

_____

_____

_____

Learning objectives	😀	😐	☹️
I can exchange coins to make different amounts.			
I can make exact sums with different coins.			
I can say how I worked out the answer to a money problem.			
I can choose units to measure and compare the length of objects.			
I can use weights and scales to work out the weight of a parcel.			
I can compare the length, weight or capacity of different objects, using the correct words.			
I know the months of the year and I can say them in order.			
I can read all the o'clock times.			
I know the order of the days of the week.			